"Lord, I Know You Need Somebody"

Dag Heward-Mills

Parchment House

"Lord, I Know You Need
Somebody"

Copyright © 2022 Dag Heward-Mills

Published by Parchment House 2022
1st Printing 2022

Find out more about Dag Heward-Mills
Healing Jesus Campaign
Write to: evangelist@daghewardmills.org
Website: www.daghewardmills.org
Facebook: Dag Heward-Mills
Twitter: @EvangelistDag

ISBN: 978-1-64330-623-0

Contents

CHAPTER 1

"Lord, I Know You Need Somebody!"

And I SOUGHT FOR A MAN among them, that should make up the hedge, and stand in the gap before me for the land, that I should not destroy it: but I found none.

Ezekiel 22:30

All through the Bible God is found looking for somebody.

All through the Bible, we find people who responded and said, "Lord, You can depend on me." Why is God looking for people?

Why would God be looking for you?

What would the Lord be needing from you?

What is it that God cannot do for himself?

What is it that God cannot achieve by Himself?

Why would Almighty God need a frail, weak, sinful human being like myself?

I am too small for God to need me!

The Mouse and the Lion

One day, the mighty lion caught a little mouse in the forest. He was about to chew on the mouse when the little mouse cried out for mercy. "Please have mercy on me and don't eat me." The mouse explained, "You don't need me. I am too small to satisfy you. I weigh only 400grams and I know that you need to eat about ten kilos of meat every day. Please don't eat me up. "But the lion answered and said, "I will eat you as a snack and not as my main meal. It will keep my hunger down till I get my main meal." But the mouse continued to plead and scream and beg the lion. The mouse said, "One day I may be able to help you. You can never tell how a nobody like me can save the king of the forest."

The lion's heart was touched and he decided to spit out the mouse and allow it to run away. "After all, this snack will not help me much," he thought.

A few months later, the lion was caught in a huge net set by a hunter. He roared and roared in dismay, frightening all the other animals in the forest. The little mouse also heard the roaring of

2

the lion and decided to come and find out what was going on. He was amazed to find out that the lion was completely intertwined and trapped within the net. The mouse said to the lion, as he climbed over the net, "I will help you to escape." He began to gnaw at the net. He chewed away several sections of the twine and made a hole for the lion to escape. The lion was so grateful to be set free by this little mouse. He was even more grateful that he had not eaten the mouse.

God and You

You are the little mouse and God is the lion! You may think there is nothing you can do for God because you are a little, weak, frail, useless, fallen creature. But there are many things that you can still do for God. God has many things that he wants you to do for Him. That is why you sense that God needs you and wants you. Today, you must open your heart and receive the call of God and say, "Lord, I know You need somebody. You can depend on me!" You must say, "Lord I hear Your call and I am ready to jump into action."

1. **Lord, I know You need somebody who will go in between God and men.**

   And I SOUGHT FOR A MAN AMONG THEM, THAT SHOULD MAKE UP THE HEDGE, and stand in the gap before me for the land, that I should not destroy it: but I found none.

                                                      Ezekiel 22:30

   God is looking for somebody who will stand in the gap! To "stand in the gap" is to stand between God and man. Instead of allowing men to encounter the wrath of God, an intercessor will stand and pray to God for mercy.

   The wrath of God that brings destruction will be averted because of the man who stands in the gap. Sometimes, the anger of a father can be redirected or soothed because of someone who intelligently speaks to the father.

All through the Bible, God is looking for somebody to stand in the gap.

Many people have answered and said, "Lord, You can depend on me. Lord, I know You need someone to stand in the gap. I am available! Please use me!"

2. Lord, I know You need somebody who will help the people of God.

In the fifteenth year of Amaziah the son of Joash king of Judah Jeroboam the son of Joash king of Israel began to reign in Samaria, and reigned forty and one years.

And he did that which was evil in the sight of the Lord: he departed not from all the sins of Jeroboam the son of Nebat, who made Israel to sin.

He restored the coast of Israel from the entering of Hamath unto the sea of the plain, according to the word of the Lord God of Israel, which he spake by the hand of his servant Jonah, the son of Amittai, the prophet, which was of Gathhepher.

FOR THE LORD SAW THE AFFLICTION OF ISRAEL, THAT IT WAS VERY BITTER: FOR THERE WAS NOT ANY SHUT UP, NOR ANY LEFT, NOR ANY HELPER FOR ISRAEL.

And the Lord said not that he would blot out the name of Israel from under heaven: but he saved them by the hand of Jeroboam the son of Joash.

2 Kings 14:23-27

God is looking for someone to help the people! People need the Lord! People need help! Everybody needs a little help to get his life together. There is no exception to this reality! If you are part of this world, you will one day need help. You will be very glad that there is someone who can help you every step of the way.

4

You will be glad that there will be someone who understands your problem. You will be happy that there will be somebody who can help you climb out of the hole where you have fallen. You will be happy to have somebody who helps you to climb down safely from the mountain where you are stuck.

Will you be the "somebody" who is sent to help someone?

"Lord I know You need somebody to help the people of God. You can use me!"

3. **Lord, I know You need somebody who can answer their questions.**

CALL NOW, IF THERE BE ANY THAT WILL ANSWER THEE; AND TO WHICH OF THE SAINTS WILT THOU TURN? For wrath killeth the foolish man, and envy slayeth the silly one.

Job 5:1-2

God is looking for someone who can answer questions! People have questions to ask. People want to understand what is happening. Why did this happen to me? Am I a good person or a bad person? Is God angry with me? Am I under a curse?

Many years ago, I entered into a prayer meeting where I heard some charismatics Christians praying. I found it so funny that I burst out laughing. I laughed and laughed at their expressions and sounds. I was not used to these expressions and sounds. I had only been to churches where there was absolute silence throughout the service. In those churches everyone prayed in their heads and no one spoke out loud.

To hear people making sounds and expressing some kind of feeling or emotion towards God whilst they were praying was a shock to me. I found it pretentious and I thought it was not real. After laughing however, I began to feel terrible. I felt I had sinned against the Holy Ghost. I became worried that I had crossed the line and committed the unpardonable sin.

It was only after I asked an older Christian that he explained to me that I had not sinned against the Holy Ghost, and that I could still be forgiven. If I had not had someone to answer my questions, I would have walked away from God and never looked back because I would have assumed that I was condemned. Thank God that there are people to answer your questions. God is looking for someone who will answer the questions of young people.

4. Lord, I know You need somebody who will deliver the children who are far from safety.

Call now, if there be any that will answer thee; and to which of the saints wilt thou turn?
For wrath killeth the foolish man, and envy slayeth the silly one. I have seen the foolish taking root: but suddenly I cursed his habitation.
HIS CHILDREN ARE FAR FROM SAFETY, AND THEY ARE CRUSHED IN THE GATE, NEITHER IS THERE ANY TO DELIVER THEM. Whose harvest the hungry eateth up, and taketh it even out of the thorns, and the robber swalloweth up their substance.

Job 5:1-5

God is looking for someone who will deliver the children who are far from safety. Many children are in danger of being swallowed up by sexual dragons. There are people who are crushed in the gate. They are hurt and stuck in the gate with one foot in and one foot out.

One day, I met a young Christian brother who had been abused as a child. He had been abused by a neighbour. Because of this, the young man had developed an unwholesome attraction for men. He was confused about his sexuality. He found girls beautiful but was still confused. When he mentioned this to me, I explained the biological, medical and spiritual realities and implications of his thoughts.

I explained to him that sexual pervasion was a sin just like fornication, stealing, jealousy and lying. Those who practice these things are entitled to their lifestyles and have a right to freely do whatever they want. I explained to him that Christians also have a human right to believe in the Bible, to preach the Bible and to practice the Bible without being vilified and ostracised for it. I explained to him that Christians have a human right to believe in the Bible, to preach the Bible and to practice the Bible without it being called hate speech or hatred. Christians also have a human right to believe in the Bible, to preach the Bible and to practice the Bible without maliciously being referred to as homophobic. I explained to him that we Christians do not hate sexual perverts and that it is unfortunate that someone would even suggest that we do.

I explained to him that human rights allow everyone to have a religion and to believe whatever they want without attacking others for their beliefs. I explained to him that Christians do not attack or hate others because of their sexual lifestyles. I explained to him that Christians preach the word of God and are allowed to repeat the words in the Bible and to declare their beliefs freely without being hated, attacked or imprisoned.

Then I answered some more questions of this young man.

He asked, "Is there sexual perversion in animals?" I said that I had not heard of any animals created on earth who were sexual perverts. I explained to him that I had also never seen two female cats or two male dogs or two male foxes or two male lions having sex before.

He asked, "Are some boys supposed to be girls?" I explained to him that every man has some female hormones and every woman has some male hormones. I also explained to him that some boys can behave girly and some girls can behave like boys.

He asked, "Can I have sex through the anus?" I explained to him that the anus was meant for the passage of faeces and not for sexual intercourse. I also added that the anal sphincter muscles would be in danger of being torn or weakened through sex and could result in him becoming incontinent of solid and liquid faeces and gas.

He asked what Sodom and Gomorrah was about. I explained to him that there are some godless modern governments who are going the way of Sodom and Gomorrah and are destroying their society and that he should not allow himself to be among those who are destroyed. I explained to him that there was a movement that had began to promote the marriage of humans and animals. Very soon people would be fighting for the rights to marry dogs, cats, foxes and mice. I explained to him that there was no need to follow something that was contrary to the Bible.

"Lord, I know You need somebody to deliver the children! Lord, I know You need somebody to help those who are not safe! I am here, Lord! Please use me!"

5. Lord, I know You need somebody who will become an intercessor between God and men.

Even if I washed myself with soap and my hands with cleansing powder, you would plunge me into a slime pit so that even my clothes would detest me. "He is not a mere mortal like me that I might answer him, that we might confront each other in court. IF ONLY THERE WERE SOMEONE TO MEDIATE BETWEEN US, SOMEONE TO BRING US TOGETHER, someone to remove God's rod from me, so that his terror would frighten me no more. Then I would speak up without fear of him, but as it now stands with me, I cannot.

Job 9:30-35 (NIV)

God is looking for someone who knows how to pray. A mediator is someone who will pray for hours and beg for the salvation of souls. No one will be saved without intercession.

8

There are a lot of people with good ideas. There are a lot of people with a good education. There are a lot of people with degrees. But there are not many people who can intercede for another. The Lord needs somebody who can pray for three hours. The Lord needs somebody who can pray for seven hours every day.

I once sent missionaries somewhere. They were not able to get good results on the mission field. I found out that they spent hours watching movies, instead of praying. The Lord is not in need of those who can watch movies. There are thousands of people who can watch movies all day long. The Lord is in need of somebody who can pray and intercede until God moves on our behalf.

"Lord, I know You need somebody to mediate for the people. Please use me as a mediator!"

6. Lord, I know You need somebody who will help people who don't have power and strength.

But Job answered and said, HOW HAST THOU HELPED HIM THAT IS WITHOUT POWER? HOW SAVEST THOU THE ARM THAT HATH NO STRENGTH?

How hast thou counselled him that hath no wisdom? And how hast thou plentifully declared the thing as it is?

Job 26:1-3

The Lord is looking for someone to help people who do not have strength. Many people know what to do! Many people know the scriptures! But many do not have the strength to do what is right.

One day I spoke to a young Christian lady who had fallen in love with a guy. As I spoke to her, I realised that she was very attached to this unbeliever guy. Her life was one of endless fornication with this guy who had no intentions of marrying her.

"Are you doing the right thing?" I asked her.

She said, "No, but I don't have the strength to stop doing it. I keep falling. I can't help myself." I knew immediately that she was without strength and power. As the scripture said, *"How hast thou helped him that is without power? How savest thou the arm that hath no strength?" (Job 26:2)* Indeed, the work of a shepherd is to help people who have no strength to do what is right. Through the counsel she received, she became strong enough to break away from this destroyer of her life.

One day, one of the sisters in the church was totally in the grips of a boyfriend. She had no strength to say "No" to this man. Her boyfriend had the keys to her apartment. She confessed that this man came and went at will and did whatever he wanted to her. The shepherd decided to help this lady who was without strength to change her situation. He went to the house with a carpenter and changed the locks on the door. Through the intervention of this shepherd, this sister without power and strength was delivered from the grips of the dragon.

"Lord, I know You need somebody to help him that is without power. Please use me!"

7. Lord, I know You need somebody who will become a father to the fatherless.

When the ear heard me, then it blessed me; and when the eye saw me, it gave witness to me: BECAUSE I DELIVERED THE POOR THAT CRIED, AND THE FATHERLESS, AND HIM THAT HAD NONE TO HELP HIM.

Job 29:11-12

God is looking for someone who will be a father to the fatherless. There are many fatherless people. There are people with absentee fathers.

One day, I met a sister who looked normal on the outside. After a while, I realised that she had an emptiness in her soul because she was fatherless. Her father had walked away from her mother when she was five years old. She did not see him again for many years. Although this sister had grown up looking normal, she lacked something that a father would give. God had sent me to be a father to her.

There are many people who need fathers. A father is a provider! A father is a guiding post! A father dictates the way for his child until the child matures out of his direct instructions. When a father is missing, there is a huge gap that is difficult to define. Without a father, many people's lives are like a boat out at sea which drifts according to the currents of the day. God is looking for people who will be fathers to the fatherless.

"Lord, I know You need somebody to become a father to the fatherless!"

8. **Lord, I know You need somebody who will deliver people from the devil who wants to rip their soul in pieces.**

O Lord my God, in thee do I put my trust: save me from all them that persecute me, and deliver me: LEST HE TEAR MY SOUL LIKE A LION, RENDING IT IN PIECES, WHILE THERE IS NONE TO DELIVER.

Psalm 7:1-2

God is looking for someone who will deliver those whose souls are torn up. A person whose soul has been torn apart by a lion! What does that mean? The lion represents the devil. The devil has destroyed people's souls. The soul consists of the mind, the will and the emotions of a person. There are people whose souls are ravaged by evil spirits. Demonised people need the Lord!

A person whose soul is ripped apart by a lion is unable to control his emotions and his will. Such people cannot stop sinning. They cannot control themselves! When they come under a little pressure, they fall helplessly. When a predator-man meets a young girl and has sexual encounters with her, he can damage her soul, her will, her emotions and her mind. The young lady may be unable to control all ensuing relationships. Gradually, she becomes a shameful strange woman who does not respect herself.

I once watched a documentary of a lady who had sex with animals. Her soul was destroyed. She went deeper and deeper into drugs, alcohol and sex with different types of animals. She eventually became a demonised wreck of a human being. She died suddenly in her middle age. These are people whom Jesus died for. Jesus loves people whose souls are ripped apart by lions.

One day, I met a Christian lady. I immediately detected the presence of two evil spirits in her. Her soul had been destroyed by spirits of fear and of pride. God is looking for someone who can care for people whose souls are destroyed by lions of pride and fear. Will you be one of the people who are ready to go and save someone?

"Lord, I know You need somebody to deliver those whose souls are torn up by lions. Here I am, send me! Here I am, use me! I will deliver Your people from the lion!"

9. Lord, I know You need somebody who will deliver people from trouble.

BE NOT FAR FROM ME; FOR TROUBLE IS NEAR; FOR THERE IS NONE TO HELP.
Many bulls have compassed me: strong bulls of Bashan have beset me round. They gaped upon me with their mouths, as a ravening and a roaring lion.

Psalm 22:11-13

God is looking for someone to deliver people who are in trouble. People need the Lord!

All through your years on this earth, you will encounter trouble. People have different reactions to trouble. Some people are destroyed by the trouble that they encounter. Others are so affected that their personality is changed.

Financial trouble, marital trouble, trouble in relationships and trouble at work are all the different types of trouble you can have. God needs someone who will show His people the way to solve problems through the help of God. Jesus is the answer for the world today!

"Lord, I know You need somebody to deliver people from their troubles. Here I am, send me!"

10. Lord, I know You need somebody who will comfort and take pity on broken-hearted people.

Thou hast known my reproach, and my shame, and my dishonour: mine adversaries are all before thee. REPROACH HATH BROKEN MY HEART; AND I AM FULL OF HEAVINESS: AND I LOOKED FOR SOME TO TAKE PITY, BUT THERE WAS NONE; AND FOR COMFORTERS, BUT I FOUND NONE. They gave me also gall for my meat; and in my thirst they gave me vinegar to drink.

Psalm 69:19-21

God is looking for somebody to help the broken-hearted. There are many problems in the world. A broken heart occurs when someone's expectations are dashed. The mental hospital has many ladies sitting on their beds calling out the names of men who promised to marry them. Their hearts are broken and the bitterness of the disappointment has overwhelmed them. A shepherd is somebody who is available to comfort a broken heart.

I was once looking after a woman whose husband had died. I was so affected by the loss of this brother that I drove this new widow around the city, comforting and consoling her. I was desperate because I did not know how to bring her husband back. I also did not know what to say. At a point, my words were finished and I began to depend on the music in the car to console the new widow. God did not expect me to bring the brother back to life. He just expected me to be there and to comfort the sister in her loss. God is looking for people who can comfort the broken-hearted.

"Lord, I know You need somebody to comfort and take pity on the broken-hearted. I am available!"

11. Lord, I know You need somebody who will deliver the needy and the poor.

FOR HE SHALL DELIVER THE NEEDY WHEN HE CRIETH; THE POOR ALSO, AND HIM THAT HATH NO HELPER.

He shall spare the poor and needy, and shall save the souls of the needy. He shall redeem their soul from deceit and violence: and precious shall their blood be in his sight.

Psalm 72:12-14

God is looking for someone to deliver the needy and the poor. There are many poor people who have no solution to their problems. I never really understood beggars till I watched a documentary on beggars in Africa. All those beggars were physically challenged. They walked around on their hands and twisted knees. One of those physically challenged persons explained on camera why he was a beggar.

He said, "If I do not beg, I will not eat."

He said, "I have no source of income whatsoever. No one gives anything to me. The government does not look after us."

I saw the terrible muddy conditions in which the beggars lived. The beggar ended his interview by saying, "I have no choice. I have to beg, otherwise I will die. My only hope is to go on the streets and beg for money." Jesus loves all these people!

It is nice that we sit in our super comfortable homes. It is a tragedy that we never understand the lives of the poor and needy. It is an even greater tragedy that we do nothing to deliver these poor and needy people.

"Lord, I know You need somebody to deliver the poor and needy. I am available!"

12. Lord, I know You need somebody who will deliver those who sit in darkness and in the shadow of death.

SUCH AS SIT IN DARKNESS AND IN THE SHADOW OF DEATH, being bound in affliction and iron; because they rebelled against the words of God, and contemned the counsel of the most High: THEREFORE HE BROUGHT DOWN THEIR HEART WITH LABOUR; THEY FELL DOWN, AND THERE WAS NONE TO HELP.

Then they cried unto the Lord in their trouble, and he saved them out of their distresses."

Psalm 107:10-13

God is looking for someone to help those who sit in the shadow of death. There are many people who sit in darkness and in the shadow of death. To sit in the shadow of death is to be near death. If you are in the shadow of death, it means you are a step away from dying. There are so many people who are on the brink of death. The fear of death has gripped them. They need someone to visit them and comfort them. When people are in the throes of death, they are frightened and grasping for hope. Will you be there to speak to them?

Will you be there when they are tormented and thinking about what they are leaving behind? Will you be there for them when they are thinking about how their funeral will be like?

I have watched several people pine away and die slowly. I visited some cancer patients just before they died, knowing that this was the last time I would ever see them. All these people need comfort and prayer.

Once, a dying and terrified man grabbed my shirt and begged me to help him go to Germany for the best medical care. I will never forget the fear and terror I saw in his eyes.

In the misery, in the sorrow, in the difficulty, there is always a need for someone who is strong, anointed and full of the word of God. God is looking for someone to do this great work for Him.

"Lord, I know You need somebody to help the people who sit in the shadow of death. Lord, You can depend on me!"

13. Lord, I know You need somebody who will be a refuge to those escaping the snare of the devil.

When my spirit was overwhelmed within me, then thou knewest my path. In the way wherein I walked have they privily laid a snare for me.
I LOOKED ON MY RIGHT HAND, AND BEHELD, BUT THERE WAS NO MAN THAT WOULD KNOW ME: REFUGE FAILED ME; NO MAN CARED FOR MY SOUL.
I cried unto thee, O Lord: I said, Thou art my refuge and my portion in the land of the living. Attend unto my cry; for I am brought very low: deliver me from my persecutors; for they are stronger than I.

Psalm 142:3-6

God is looking for someone to be a refuge. Today, there are people who cannot give their lives to Christ without being hounded by their families. Sometimes, these newly-converted individuals need a refuge, a place where they can hide. It is time for someone to rise up and be a refuge for the new converts.

Your church is a refuge! It is a place where people find a place to hide. Sometimes a home is a place of temptation and difficulty. It is time to build a church that will be a refuge for those who are being saved.

14. Lord, I know You need somebody who will comfort the weak and oppressed.

Then I looked again at all the acts of oppression, which were being done under the sun. And behold I SAW THE

16

TEARS OF THE OPPRESSED AND THAT THEY HAD
NO ONE TO COMFORT THEM; and on the side of their
oppressors was power, but they had no one to comfort
them.

Ecclesiastes 4:1 (NASB)

*God is looking for someone to comfort the weak and the
oppressed.* Human beings have been born into a world of
oppression. Many human beings are weak. There are always
two groups of people in the world: the weak and the strong, the
powerful and the feeble, those who are up and those who are
down, the rich and the poor, the educated and the uneducated.
Unfortunately, the strong, powerful and rich people in the world
oppress those who are less fortunate. Almighty God sees all
the acts of oppression that are being meted out to people. He is
looking for someone who can comfort the oppressed.

Perhaps, you may never know how blessed you are to read
this book and be among the people who can help to deliver the
oppressed. The fact that you are reading this book means that
you are in a certain category of people. Open your eyes and
look around. You will see many people who need help and
deliverance from oppression.

All through history, the powerful have oppressed the weak.
When the white man had control over the black man, he
oppressed him and made him yearn for freedom. When men
had power over women, they oppressed them until they longed
to be equal to men. When the educated and the rich had power
over the masses, the poor people of the world formed unions to
fight for themselves to be delivered from the unreasonable and
wicked elite.

When kings had power over peasants, they oppressed them,
executed them and crushed them until the poor and oppressed
peoples of the world did away with kings.

Oppression is a part of human existence. Any group that gets
the upper hand will oppress the weaker, and that without fail.
That is why human rights are a big thing in the world today.

Please open your eyes! You will see people who are subject to oppression for one reason or the other. They are pressed down and beaten in every unreasonable way. In marriage, the husband or the wife may have the upper hand. Usually, the partner with the upper hand oppresses the partner who does not have much of a choice.

15. Lord, I know You need somebody who will deliver people from Your anger.

THEREFORE IS THE ANGER OF THE LORD KINDLED AGAINST HIS PEOPLE, AND HE HATH STRETCHED FORTH HIS HAND AGAINST THEM, AND HATH SMITTEN THEM: AND THE HILLS DID TREMBLE, AND THEIR CARCASES WERE TORN IN THE MIDST OF THE STREETS. FOR ALL THIS HIS ANGER IS NOT TURNED AWAY, BUT HIS HAND IS STRETCHED OUT STILL.

And he will lift up an ensign to the nations from far, and will hiss unto them from the end of the earth: and, behold, they shall come with speed swiftly: None shall be weary nor stumble among them; none shall slumber nor sleep; neither shall the girdle of their loins be loosed, nor the latchet of their shoes be broken: Whose arrows are sharp, and all their bows bent, their horses' hoofs shall be counted like flint, and their wheels like a whirlwind: Their roaring shall be like a lion, they shall roar like young lions: yea, they shall roar, and lay hold of the prey, and shall carry it away safe, and none shall deliver it.

And in that day they shall roar against them like the roaring of the sea: and if one look unto the land, behold darkness and sorrow, and the light is darkened in the heavens thereof.

Isaiah 5:25-30

God is looking for someone to deliver people from His anger. God gets angry and when He does, His wrath is not easy to bear. It takes a lot for God's wrath to be kindled against you. You must have done a lot for the anger of the Lord to rise up against you. When the anger of the Lord is kindled against you, you will experience divine judgments that are supernatural in their very nature. God's anger is kindled against people when their cups are full. The reason why God's anger and judgment does not come every day is because God is just and fair. He allows your cup to be full! "But in the fourth generation they shall come hither again: for the iniquity of the Amorites is not yet full" (Genesis 15:16).

Do not think that God never gets angry. The goodness of God is supposed to lead you to repentance. Many people are on the brink of God's wrath and judgment. The iniquity of the Amorites was not full and that is why they were allowed to carry on as though nothing was wrong. You will notice many scriptures that speak of the anger of God as though it is a cup full of wine. The cup has to be full for judgment to flow.

> The same shall drink of the wine of the wrath of God, which is poured out without mixture into the cup of his indignation; and he shall be tormented with fire and brimstone in the presence of the holy angels, and in the presence of the Lamb:
>
> Revelation 14:10

God is calling you to intervene in people's lives. God is calling you to intervene in the lives of people who are just about to experience the anger of God in their lives. Sodom and Gomorrah were on the brink of God's judgment. Abraham was the last roadblock on their way to destruction. Abraham was able to negotiate a deal for the people of Sodom and Gomorrah. Unfortunately, the people of Sodom and Gomorrah could not prevent the rain of fire, brimstone and terror.

16. Lord, I know You need somebody who will bring good tidings to Your people.

> Behold, ye are of nothing, and your work of nought: an abomination is he that chooseth you. I have raised up one from the north, and he shall come: from the rising of

the sun shall he call upon my name: and he shall come upon princes as upon morter, and as the potter treadeth clay. Who hath declared from the beginning, that we may know? And beforetime, that we may say, He is righteous? yea, there is none that sheweth, yea, there is none that declareth, yea, there is none that heareth your words. The first shall say to Zion, BEHOLD, BEHOLD THEM: AND I WILL GIVE TO JERUSALEM ONE THAT BRINGETH GOOD TIDINGS. For I beheld, and there was no man; even among them, and there was no counsellor, that, when I asked of them, could answer a WORD.

Isaiah 41:24-28

God is looking for someone who will bring good tidings to people. What are good tidings? Good tidings are good news. It is news of the salvation of Jesus Christ that has come to the world. When a nation receives the good news of Jesus Christ, the nation is changed forever. The nations that have been visited by evangelists are different from nations that have never received such visits. I have visited nations in Africa that have never had an evangelist visit them. These nations have few churches and very little light. Some of these nations are so far back that they did not understand what an evangelistic campaign was.

In one nation I visited, the people thought the crusade was a drinking party. In the evening, when the lights and music of the crusade began, the people came with their girlfriends and their alcoholic drinks to the crusade ground. They thought it was a party where they could get drunk and have sex. It took a long time to gain control of this rowdy crowd who had never before set eyes on an evangelist bringing good tidings.

It is so sad to visit such nations because they are so lost without the gospel of Jesus Christ. Such places have very few churches and few Christians.

Ghana is a nation which has had the privilege of receiving visiting evangelists like Billy Graham, Reinhard Bonnke, Benny Hinn, T. L. Osborne and Morris Cerullo.

God is looking for people who are going to bring good tidings. God is sending someone to bring good tidings. That person is you! Will you take up the call?

17. Lord, I know You need somebody who will deliver and restore people who have been held captive by the enemy.

The Lord is well pleased for his righteousness' sake; he will magnify the law, and make it honourable.

BUT THIS IS A PEOPLE ROBBED AND SPOILED; THEY ARE ALL OF THEM SNARED IN HOLES, AND THEY ARE HID IN PRISON HOUSES: THEY ARE FOR A PREY, AND NONE DELIVERETH; FOR A SPOIL, AND NONE SAITH, RESTORE.

Who among you will give ear to this? who will hearken and hear for the time to come?

Who gave Jacob for a spoil, and Israel to the robbers? did not the LORD, he against whom we have sinned? for they would not walk in his ways, neither were they obedient unto his law.

Therefore he hath poured upon him the fury of his anger, and the strength of battle: and it hath set him on fire round about, yet he knew not; and it burned him, yet he laid it not to heart.

Isaiah 42:21-25

God is looking for someone who will deliver and restore people who have been held captive by the enemy. There are people who have been robbed and spoiled. Many young people are robbed of their purity. They are robbed of their virginity. Many people are sexually violated and robbed. Unfortunately, there are pastors who also rob and spoil people's lives. How does a person spoil someone's life? When you introduce someone to sexual perversity, the person is changed forever.

Sexual perversion, for instance, is something that can be introduced to a young, tender and innocent person. After the person is baptised into this behaviour, his orientation is changed and he is unable to be normal any longer. He is never sure what he is, after his youthful encounter with a robber and a spoiler.

Also, when a girl is introduced into deception, fornication and immorality, she can grow up practicing these things at the least opportunity she has. Instead of growing up as a sweet, innocent, tender and pure lady, she grows up perverted, immoral and wicked.

Through your presence and your intervention, robbers and spoilers will be stopped in their tracks. People's lives and families will be saved. People's personalities will be saved from becoming perverted and confused.

God is looking for shepherds who will intervene and stand between the robber and the young girl.

Someone who will stand between the spoiler and the young man! Will you be a shepherd? Wouldn't you like someone to save your little daughter or your son? Do not sit there as though you cannot do anything. God is looking for someone to work for him and to care for people.

"Lord, I know You need somebody!"

18. Lord, I know You need somebody who will plead for You to stay Your judgment on those who deserve punishment.

Who is this that cometh from Edom, with dyed garments from Bozrah? This that is glorious in his apparel, travelling in the greatness of his strength? I that speak in righteousness, mighty to save.
Wherefore art thou red in thine apparel, and thy garments like him that treadeth in the winefat?
I have trodden the winepress alone; and of the people there was none with me: for I will tread them in mine anger, and trample them in my fury; and their blood shall be sprinkled upon my garments, and I will stain all my raiment.
For the day of vengeance is in mine heart, and the year of my redeemed is come.

AND I LOOKED, AND THERE WAS NONE TO HELP;
AND I WONDERED THAT THERE WAS NONE TO
UPHOLD: THEREFORE MINE OWN ARM BROUGHT
SALVATION UNTO ME; AND MY FURY, IT UPHELD
ME.

Isaiah 63:1-5

God is looking for someone to help. Everybody needs a little help to get his life together. God sent the Holy Spirit to our lives to be a helper. No one can make it in this life without help. When Jesus was on the road to Calvary, carrying His cross, Simon of Cyrene came to help Him carry the cross. Even Jesus needed help to carry the cross! How much more ordinary people like us? We will all need someone who will help us carry our crosses. You will need someone to help you take up your cross and go on the mission. You will need someone to help you take up your cross and stop living with that boyfriend. You will need someone to help you break out of bad relationships that are only harmful to your life.

There are many people who know that they must obey God. Many of these people need a little help to get themselves going. Are you going to be that person who will help them?

God is looking for someone to help. He is amazed as he looks and finds no one to help. "And I looked, and there was none to help; and I wondered that there was none to uphold: therefore mine own arm brought salvation unto me; and my fury, it upheld me." (Isaiah 63:5).

19. Lord, I know You need somebody who will pray for the healing of those whose lovers have forsaken them.

Therefore fear thou not, O my servant Jacob, saith the LORD; neither be dismayed, O Israel: for, lo, I will save thee from afar, and thy seed from the land of their captivity; and Jacob shall return, and shall be in rest, and be quiet, and none shall make him afraid.
For I am with thee, saith the LORD, to save thee: though I

make a full end of all nations whither I have scattered thee, yet will I not make a full end of thee: but I will correct thee in measure, and will not leave thee altogether unpunished. For thus saith the LORD, Thy bruise is incurable, and thy wound is grievous.

THERE IS NONE TO PLEAD THY CAUSE, THAT THOU MAYEST BE BOUND UP: THOU HAST NO HEALING MEDICINES.

ALL THY LOVERS HAVE FORGOTTEN THEE; they seek thee not; for I have wounded thee with the wound of an enemy, with the chastisement of a cruel one, for the multitude of thine iniquity; because thy sins were increased.

Jeremiah 30:10-14

God is looking for someone to care for people whose lovers have forsaken them. There is a time when a person encounters many deceptive lovers. In time of trouble, these wicked "lovers" run away and desert the person. There are many ladies who have had numerous lovers. These numerous lovers have had a jolly time playing with their victims. When something tragic happens to their victim, these lovers scatter and leave her abandoned, lonely and wounded.

There are many unmarried ladies who look as though they have never been loved. Indeed, many of them have been loved by untold numbers of hunters and seekers of pleasure. You would be amazed at the number of people that have passed through their lives. Unfortunately, as time passes, all these dishonourable men become deserters.

God is sending you with healing medicines to minister to the dejected, forlorn lady who has no more lovers. She is praying every day for someone to come along and marry her. She is now ready to turn to God and live a sober life away from these users of her body.

If you reach out to her with the healing medicine of the word of God, she will be healed and bound by the spiritual help you give her.

"Lord, I know You need somebody to help bring healing to the forsaken woman."

20. Lord, I know You need somebody who will help those who have fallen into the hands of the enemy.

How doth the city sit solitary, that was full of people! How is she become as a widow! She that was great among the nations, and princess among the provinces, how is she become tributary!

She weepeth sore in the night, and her tears are on her cheeks: among all her lovers she hath none to comfort her: all her friends have dealt treacherously with her, they are become her enemies.

Judah is gone into captivity because of affliction, and because of great servitude: she dwelleth among the heathen, she findeth no rest: all her persecutors overtook her between the straits.

The ways of Zion do mourn, because none come to the solemn feasts: all her gates are desolate: her priests sigh, her virgins are afflicted, and she is in bitterness.

Her adversaries are the chief, her enemies prosper; for the LORD hath afflicted her for the multitude of her transgressions: her children are gone into captivity before the enemy.

And from the daughter of Zion all her beauty is departed: her princes are become like harts that find no pasture, and they are gone without strength before the pursuer.

Jerusalem remembered in the days of her affliction and of her miseries all her pleasant things that she had in the days of old, WHEN HER PEOPLE FELL INTO THE HAND OF THE ENEMY, AND NONE DID HELP HER: the adversaries saw her, and did mock at her sabbaths.

Lamentations 1:1-7

God is looking for someone who will help those who have

fallen into the hands of the enemy. Many people have fallen into the hands of the enemy. Perhaps, through some unfortunate circumstances, a child of God has fallen into the hands of the enemy. The enemy would like to kill the child of God. The enemy will never let the child of God go free. When people fall into the hands of the enemy, they are in the hands of a strong man. "When a strong man armed keepeth his palace, his goods are in peace: But when a stronger than he shall come upon him, and overcome him, he taketh from him all his armour wherein he trusted, and divideth his spoils" (Luke 11:21-22).

The strong man is the enemy of God. He has captured the people and God is sending you to deliver the people from captivity. You are the one who is stronger than he. God declares you to be stronger than satan! You are anointed to deliver them from the enemy.

"Lord, I know You need somebody to deliver Your people who have fallen into the hands of the enemy and are being guarded in the enemy's palace."

21. Lord, I know You need somebody who will deliver people from reproach and other evil things they need not suffer.

Remember, O LORD, what is come upon us: consider, and behold our reproach. Our inheritance is turned to strangers, our houses to aliens. We are orphans and fatherless, our mothers are as widows.

We have drunken our water for money; our wood is sold unto us. Our necks are under persecution: we labour, and have no rest. We have given the hand to the Egyptians, and to the Assyrians, to be satisfied with bread.

Our fathers have sinned, and are not; and we have borne their iniquities. SERVANTS HAVE RULED OVER US: THERE IS NONE THAT DOTH DELIVER US OUT OF THEIR HAND.

Lamentations 5:1-8

God is looking for someone deliver people from reproach and other evils. When servants rule, the nation trembles. When servants rule, there is a lot of confusion, poverty and mismanagement. When servants rule, there is a lot of shabbiness, filth, dirt and ugliness in the environment. When servants rule, there is a general inability to move forward.

When servants rule, there is an inability to take decisions. When servants rule, there is no financial security for anyone. When servants rule, there is total dependency on hand-outs, gifts and loans from an external source.

When servants rule, grandiose plans are presented but there is no ability to implement or execute these plans. When servants are in charge, there are lots of festivities, parties and anniversary celebrations. The servant is so glad that he is finally a leader that he gives himself to endless merriment and revelries.

When servants rule, there is disorganisation. When servants rule, there are a lot of meetings, conferences and seminars but no action is ever taken. When servants rule, there is a lot of waste. Servants do not know how to save things because they have never had to create or build anything.

When servants rule, there is no building project. When servants rule, there are a lot of speeches but no development. When servants rule, there is a lot of dependence on consultants and other professionals. Servants do not know what to do so they need lots of consultants and professionals to delegate the complicated tasks to. These servants do not themselves understand any of the jobs that the professionals will do. Servants who rule, feel that they have been elevated, so they never roll up their sleeves and do any practical work.

Indeed, everyone born under such rule is usually poor. "For out of prison he cometh to reign; whereas also he that is born in his kingdom becometh poor" (Ecclesiastes 4:14). God is looking for people who will be good leaders and deliver people who are led by such servant-rulers.

22. Lord, I know You need somebody who will to raise up the fallen virgins.

Hear ye this word which I take up against you, even a lamentation, O house of Israel. THE VIRGIN OF ISRAEL IS FALLEN; SHE SHALL NO MORE RISE: SHE IS FORSAKEN UPON HER LAND; THERE IS NONE TO RAISE HER UP.

Amos 5:1-2

God is looking for someone to raise up the fallen virgins. Sometimes, people lose their virginity without intending to. There are many virgins who had no intention of having sex with any one. They did not even know what sex was about. But they encountered sexual predators and were slain. A man can also encounter a sexual predator and be slain. Such fallen virgins can be broken for the rest of their lives because they feel robbed and violated. Some people cannot recover from being fallen virgins.

God wants to send someone to raise up the fallen virgins. They are broken! They are dejected! They need to hear from God! You are the one who can minister the word of life to the fallen virgins.

"Lord, I know You need somebody to send to these fallen virgins. You can depend on me! I'll be there when you need me."

23. Lord, I know You need labourers and shepherds to gather the scattered flock.

And Jesus went about all the cities and villages, teaching in their synagogues, and preaching the gospel of the kingdom, and healing every sickness and every disease among the people.
BUT WHEN HE SAW THE MULTITUDES, HE WAS MOVED WITH COMPASSION ON THEM, BECAUSE THEY FAINTED, AND WERE SCATTERED ABROAD, AS SHEEP HAVING NO SHEPHERD.

28

Then saith he unto his disciples, the harvest truly is plenteous, but the labourers are few; Pray ye therefore the Lord of the harvest, that he will send forth labourers into his harvest.

Matthew 9:35-38

God is looking for labourers and shepherds to gather the scattered flock. A shepherd is a very important office in the ministry. The people are scattered because there is no shepherd. They are not scattered because there is no prophet. They are not scattered because there is no evangelist. They are scattered because there is no shepherd.

The shepherd is the one who is going to bring them together. By bringing God's people together, they are strengthened and they are established. "They go from strength to strength, every one of them in Zion appeareth before God" (Psalm 84:7)

Every time God's people meet they are strengthened. They grow from strength to strength. God is looking for someone to gather everyone together in such a way that they will become stronger. Truly, all troubled people are blessed and healed when they are in the presence of their shepherd who gathered them.

Ask ye of the LORD rain in the time of the latter rain; so the LORD shall make bright clouds, and give them showers of rain, to every one grass in the field.

For the idols have spoken vanity, and the diviners have seen a lie, and have told false dreams; they comfort in vain: THEREFORE THEY WENT THEIR WAY AS A FLOCK, THEY WERE TROUBLED, BECAUSE THERE WAS NO SHEPHERD.

Zechariah 10:1-2

Another important role of the shepherd is to prevent them from becoming meat for the wolves and other beasts in the wilderness. There are many wolves that look longingly at God's people, seeking to devour them. God wants to use you to prevent

29

people from becoming meat to the beasts and monsters out there. There are monsters who want to destroy innocent lives and you must be there to stop them.

"And the word of the LORD came unto me, saying, Son of man, prophesy against the shepherds of Israel, prophesy, and say unto them, Thus saith the Lord GOD unto the shepherds; Woe be to the shepherds of Israel that do feed themselves! should not the shepherds feed the flocks? Ye eat the fat, and ye clothe you with the wool, ye kill them that are fed: but ye feed not the flock. The diseased have ye not strengthened, neither have ye healed that which was sick, neither have ye bound up that which was broken, neither have ye brought again that which was driven away, neither have ye sought that which was lost; but with force and with cruelty have ye ruled them. AND THEY WERE SCATTERED, BECAUSE THERE IS NO SHEPHERD: AND THEY BECAME MEAT TO ALL THE BEASTS OF THE FIELD, WHEN THEY WERE SCATTERED. My sheep wandered through all the mountains, and upon every high hill: yea, my flock was scattered upon all the face of the earth, and none did search or seek after them" (Ezekiel 34:1-6).

CHAPTER 2

"Lord, You Can Depend on Me!"

...Whom shall I send, and who will go for us? Then said I, HERE AM I; SEND ME.

Isaiah 6:8

1. Lord, You can depend on me because I am saying, "Here I am, send me."

In the year that king Uzziah died I saw also the Lord sitting upon a throne, high and lifted up, and his train filled the temple.

Above it stood the seraphims: each one had six wings; with twain he covered his face, and with twain he covered his feet, and with twain he did fly.

And one cried unto another, and said, Holy, holy, holy, is the LORD of hosts: the whole earth is full of his glory.

And the posts of the door moved at the voice of him that cried, and the house was filled with smoke.

Then said I, Woe is me! for I am undone; because I am a man of unclean lips, and I dwell in the midst of a people of unclean lips: for mine eyes have seen the King, the LORD of hosts.

Then flew one of the seraphims unto me, having a live coal in his hand, which he had taken with the tongs from off the altar:

And he laid it upon my mouth, and said, Lo, this hath touched thy lips; and thine iniquity is taken away, and thy sin purged.

ALSO I HEARD THE VOICE OF THE LORD, SAYING, WHOM SHALL I SEND, AND WHO WILL GO FOR US? THEN SAID I, HERE AM I; SEND ME.

Isaiah 6:1-8

Why can God depend on you? God can depend on you because you are saying: "Here am I, send me." What you say is very important!

You are saying: "Here am I, send me."

You could have said: "Here am I, send them!" God has great hopes in you because you willingly asked God to send you away on a mission.

You could have said: "I have no time for no mission!"

You could have said: "I am not going to no world to preach no gospel!"

You could have said: "I cannot be a witness to any uttermost part of the world!"

You could have said: "I have a family and children to take care of. I cannot go on any spurious adventures!"

You could have said: "Let someone else do it! I am not the lamb of God who should sacrifice himself for the world."

By saying the words, "Here am I, send me," you are telling God to take over your life and use you.

"Here am I, send me," are blessed words. God loves it when you say, "Here am I, send me."

2. Lord, You can depend on me because I have a willing heart.

And Moses spake unto all the congregation of the children of Israel, saying, this is the thing which the Lord commanded, saying, TAKE YE FROM AMONG YOU AN OFFERING UNTO THE LORD: WHOSOEVER IS OF A WILLING HEART, LET HIM BRING IT, AN OFFERING OF THE LORD; gold, and silver, and brass,

And blue, and purple, and scarlet, and fine linen, and goats' hair,

And rams' skins dyed red, and badgers' skins, and shittim wood,

And oil for the light, and spices for anointing oil, and for the sweet incense,

And onyx stones, and stones to be set for the ephod, and for the breastplate.

Exodus 35:4-9

"Lord, You can depend on me because I have a willing heart."

Your willingness is the most beautiful part of you. An unwilling person is an ugly person. When someone does something unwillingly, it stinks.

It is time to bring a willing offering to the Lord. Your willingness makes you beautiful. Your unwillingness makes your gift unpleasant and undesirable. Beauty is vain and charm is deceitful. A willing and cheerful woman is of great value.

3. Lord, You can depend on me because my heart is stirred up.

AND THEY CAME, EVERY ONE WHOSE HEART STIRRED HIM UP, AND EVERY ONE WHOM HIS SPIRIT MADE WILLING, AND THEY BROUGHT THE LORD'S OFFERING to the work of the tabernacle of the congregation, and for all his service, and for the holy garments.

Exodus 35:21

My heart is stirred up to serve the Lord. A heart that is stirred up is of greater value than a mind that is stirred up.

God wants you to serve Him with your heart. Thank God for your stirred up mind and body! God wants something deeper than that! He wants your heart! It is time to offer yourself from your heart!

Would you like to marry someone who gives you his mind and his body but whose heart is elsewhere? Where is your heart? Allow the Lord to touch your heart and stir it up for His service.

4. Lord, You can depend on me because I am offering myself today.

Then sang Deborah and Barak the son of Abinoam on that day, saying, PRAISE YE THE LORD FOR THE AVENGING OF ISRAEL, WHEN THE PEOPLE WILLINGLY OFFERED THEMSELVES.

Hear, O ye kings; give ear, O ye princes; I, even I, will sing unto the LORD; I will sing praise to the LORD God of Israel.

Judges 5:1-3

In the days of Shamgar the son of Anath, in the days of Jael, the highways were unoccupied, and the travellers walked through byways.

The inhabitants of the villages ceased, they ceased in Israel, until that I Deborah arose, that I arose a mother in Israel.

They chose new gods; then was war in the gates: was there a shield or spear seen among forty thousand in Israel?

MY HEART IS TOWARD THE GOVERNORS OF ISRAEL, THAT OFFERED THEMSELVES WILLINGLY AMONG THE PEOPLE. Bless ye the Lord.

Judges 5:6-9

The greatest offering you can give is yourself. Thank God for the hundred dollars and the thousand dollars you give to the Lord. What about giving yourself?

I once met a man who had his thumb cut off by a machine. This man was quite happy to have lost his thumb because he earned eight thousand British pounds for his thumb.

If a thumb costs eight thousand pounds, how much do you think an arm costs? If a thumb costs eight thousand pounds, how much do you think a heart, a kidney or a liver costs? Indeed, the value of your whole body must be millions of dollars.

Imagine if a man was to give his whole body and life! How much money would he get from that?

Sometimes when aeroplanes crash, the families are paid millions of dollars for the loss of their loved ones. That shows you how valuable one human being is.

"Lord, I know You need somebody. You can depend on me because I am ready to give *myself* as an offering today."

5. Lord, You can depend on me because I am willing to use any skill I possess.

And David said to Solomon his son, Be strong and of good courage, and do it: fear not, nor be dismayed: for the Lord God, even my God, will be with thee; he will not fail thee, nor forsake thee, until thou hast finished all the work for the service of the house of the Lord.

And, behold, the courses of the priests and the Levites, even they shall be with thee for all the service of the house of God: and there shall be with thee for all manner of workmanship EVERY WILLING SKILFUL MAN, for any manner of service: also the princes and all the people will be wholly at thy commandment.

1 Chronicles 28:20-21

"Lord, You can depend on me because I am willing to use any skill I possess."

What skills do you have? It is time to deploy them for the house of God.

Is it computer skills? Is it acting skills? Is it singing skills? Is it musical skills? Is it speaking skills? It is time for you to deploy all your skills in the house of God.

Why do you sit there acting deaf and dumb? Why do you act as if you do not know how to do anything? How come you only use your organising, rallying and speaking skills for secular things? It is time to serve the Lord with all your skills.

"Lord, You can depend on me because I am willing to use *every single skill* I possess for You!"

6. Lord, You can depend on me because I have set my affection on the house of God.

MOREOVER, BECAUSE I HAVE SET MY AFFECTION TO THE HOUSE OF MY GOD, I have of mine own proper good, of gold and silver, which I have given to the house of my God, over and above all that I have prepared for the holy house,

Even three thousand talents of gold, of the gold of Ophir, and seven thousand talents of refined silver, to overlay the walls of the houses withal:

The gold for things of gold, and the silver for things of silver, and for all manner of work to be made by the hands of artificers. And who then is willing to consecrate his service this day unto the LORD?

Then the chief of the fathers and princes of the tribes of Israel, and the captains of thousands and of hundreds, with the rulers of the king's work, offered willingly,

And gave for the service of the house of God of gold five thousand talents and ten thousand drams, and of silver ten thousand talents, and of brass eighteen thousand talents, and one hundred thousand talents of iron.

1 Chronicles 29:3-7

"Lord, You can depend on me because I have set my affection on the house of God.

I am in love with the house of God.

I like the church!

I like working in the church!

I like staying in church all day long!

Lord, I have fallen in love with Your house!

Lord, I do not have any affection for the bank, the law firms, the universities, the hospitals or for the market place. My affection is fixed on the house of God!"

7. **Lord, You can depend on me because I am willing to go where You wish.**

Now this is the copy of the letter that the king Artaxerxes gave unto Ezra the priest, the scribe, even a scribe of the words of the commandments of the Lord, and of his statutes to Israel.

Artaxerxes, king of kings, unto Ezra the priest, a scribe of the law of the God of heaven, perfect peace, and at such a time.

I MAKE A DECREE, THAT ALL THEY OF THE PEOPLE OF ISRAEL, AND OF HIS PRIESTS AND LEVITES, IN MY REALM, WHICH ARE MINDED OF THEIR OWN FREEWILL TO GO UP TO JERUSALEM, GO WITH THEE.

Ezra 7:11-13

"Lord, You can depend on me because I am willing to go anywhere."

In the scripture above, we see how people were prepared to go willingly to Jerusalem to serve the Lord. There are people who go on journeys unwillingly.

It is time for you to go willingly to where God wants you to be.

"Lord, I know You need somebody to go willingly and happily to every destination on earth. I am ready to go willingly and happily to every destination in the world."

8. Lord, You can depend on me because I am willing to dwell wherever You want.

And the rulers of the people dwelt at Jerusalem: the rest of the people also cast lots, to bring one of ten to dwell in Jerusalem the holy city, and nine parts to dwell in other cities.

AND THE PEOPLE BLESSED ALL THE MEN, THAT WILLINGLY OFFERED THEMSELVES TO DWELL AT JERUSALEM.

Now these are the chief of the province that dwelt in Jerusalem: but in the cities of Judah dwelt every one in his possession in their cities, to wit, Israel, the priests, and the Levites, and the Nethinims, and the children of Solomon's servants.

Nehemiah 11:1-3

"Lord, You can depend on me because I am willing to live anywhere."

Some people are not prepared to live anywhere.

One day, I met an American missionary who lived in Ghana. He had lived in Ghana and Nigeria for many years. When I visited his home in a village in Ghana, he had about eight African children running around in his living room.

He told me: "My wife and I do not have any children of our own. We have adopted all these children." I was amazed and stunned.

Then he described how they had built a home and lived in a clearing in the middle of a forest. Wow! I exclaimed. He went on to describe how he had killed a snake that came to eat one of his chickens in the night.

Indeed, this is a man who was ready to dwell anywhere, even in the midst of a frightening forest. Are you ready to live anywhere because of your love for the Lord?

"Lord, I know You need somebody who is ready to dwell anywhere."

9. Lord, You can depend on me because I am willing to fight enemies.

The Lord shall send the rod of thy strength out of Zion: RULE THOU IN THE MIDST OF THINE ENEMIES. THY PEOPLE SHALL BE WILLING IN THE DAY OF THY POWER, in the beauties of holiness from the womb of the morning: thou hast the dew of thy youth.

The Lord hath sworn, and will not repent, Thou art a priest for ever after the order of Melchizedek.

Psalm 110:2-4

"Lord, You can depend on me because I am willing to fight the enemies."

Are you ready to go to war?

You must be ready to fight!

You must be ready to fight for a long time.

You must be ready to have enemies!

You must be ready to have nasty enemies whom you do not like.

You must be ready to be wounded because of your fights for Jesus.

There are some people who value their good image so much that they do not want to get involved in the wars of ministry.

"Lord, You can depend on me. I am ready to fight tooth and nail for Your name's sake.

I am ready to hate and be hated for Your name's sake.

I am ready to take on all those that hate Your name.

I am ready to take on all those that are lifted up against Your name, Your church and Your glory."

10. Lord, You can depend on me because I am willing and obedient.

Come now, and let us reason together, saith the LORD: though your sins be as scarlet, they shall be as white as snow; though they be red like crimson, they shall be as wool.

IF YE BE WILLING AND OBEDIENT, YE SHALL EAT
THE GOOD OF THE LAND: But if ye refuse and rebel,
ye shall be devoured with the sword: for the mouth of the
LORD hath spoken it.

Isaiah 1:18-20

"Lord, You can depend on me because I am willing and
obedient."

There are many people who are willing but not obedient.
What does God want you to do? It is not enough to be obedient.
You must be willing also! It is not enough to be willing without
being obedient.

I know missionaries who were willing to give their all to
Jesus. But they were not obedient to the instructions they were
given when they were sent out. Willingness alone will not
produce results. Eagerness and readiness are good signs. But
without obedience, there will be no fruits.

There are people who say to the Lord: "I will not go". But later
on, they go willingly and are very obedient to every instruction.
I always remember a man of God who said God had told him: "If
you want to be successful in the ministry, you must be obedient
in small things and big things." Thank God for your willingness
but thank God even more for your willingness and obedience.

"Lord, You can depend on me because I am *willing and
obedient.*"

11. Lord, You can depend on me because I preach the gospel willingly.

For though I preach the gospel, I have nothing to glory
of: for necessity is laid upon me; yea, woe is unto me, if I
preach not the gospel!
FOR IF I DO THIS THING WILLINGLY, I HAVE
A REWARD: BUT IF AGAINST MY WILL, A
DISPENSATION OF THE GOSPEL IS COMMITTED
UNTO ME.

What is my reward then? Verily that, when I preach the gospel, I may make the gospel of Christ without charge, that I abuse not my power in the gospel.

1 Corinthians 9:16-18

"Lord, You can depend on me because I preach the gospel willingly."

The gospel is the good news of Jesus Christ. Some people are happier to preach about leadership, finances, success and happiness in marriage than they are to preach the gospel. Some people think that the gospel is too simple.

Some people think that the gospel is abstract and unhelpful in the light of present-day problems.

They say, "We need to be practical and we need to help the people of this world with vocational studies, job creation, health and education."

These are nice things but they are not the gospel.

It is time to see the relevance, the beauty and the glory of the gospel of Jesus Christ. The story of the cross and the power of the blood of Jesus are the best news for this dying world. There is nothing more relevant, more practical and more life changing than the gospel of Jesus Christ.

"Lord, I am ready to preach this gospel willingly!"

12. Lord, You can depend on me because I am willing to give my soul.

But we were gentle among you, even as a nurse cherisheth her children: So being affectionately desirous of you, WE WERE WILLING TO HAVE IMPARTED UNTO YOU, NOT THE GOSPEL OF GOD ONLY, BUT ALSO OUR OWN SOULS, because ye were dear unto us. For ye remember, brethren, our labour and travail: for labouring night and day, because we would not be chargeable unto any of you, we preached unto you the gospel of God.

1 Thessalonians 2:7-9

You can depend on someone when he is doing something with his soul. Your soul is your life! When you are ready to give your soul, you are ready to give your life. Lord, Y6ou can depend on me because I am willing to give my soul. What are you holding back? There are some lifeless ministers and priests of the gospel who are a negative advertisement for becoming a minister of Christ.

You must be in the ministry with your soul, your passion and your zeal. Nothing is too hard, nowhere is too far, nothing is too difficult for you when your soul is into something.

I once met a man who told me his vision was to plant nightclubs in many cities. He described a nightclub he had in the city of Accra and another one he had in another city. He was so proud of his achievement of building nightclubs.

He was full of a passion for creating nightclubs! His soul was involved in his dream!

"Lord, I know You need somebody who is ready to give his soul for the work of God."

I once met a man who was very unimpressed with his pastor's secularized sermon. He said his pastor had read out the message instead of preaching from his heart. He felt the pastor was not ministering from his soul.

He continued, "I might as well listen to a speech given by the president instead of listening to this lifeless secularized message by my pastor."

Amazing! Even humans notice when you are not doing things from deep within.

"Lord, You can depend on me because I am gong to work for You with my soul!"

13. Lord, You can depend on me because I will do more than You say.

If thou count me therefore a partner, receive him as myself. If he hath wronged thee, or oweth thee ought, put that on mine account; I Paul have written it with mine own hand, I will repay it: albeit I do not say to thee how thou owest unto me even thine own self besides.
Yea, brother, let me have joy of thee in the Lord: refresh my bowels in the Lord.
HAVING CONFIDENCE IN THY OBEDIENCE I WROTE UNTO THEE, KNOWING THAT THOU WILT ALSO DO MORE THAN I SAY.

Philemon 1:17-21

"Lord, You can depend on me because I will do more than You say. Thank You for the instruction You have given me, but I will go the extra mile."

Would you not like to work with someone who will do more than you ask?

Why don't you make yourself someone who goes the extra mile?

What is the point when you do the barest minimum?

What is the point when you go to places just to mark the register and to show that you were there?

You will not always get away with doing the barest minimum. God sees your heart! Whatever you do, you are doing it unto the Lord. It is time to give yourself unreservedly to the gospel of Jesus Christ. Do even more than God has asked you! Be obedient! Go the extra mile for Jesus!

"Lord, You can depend on me because I will go the extra mile! I will do more than You say!"

CHAPTER 3

"Lord, People Can't See the Gift in Me"

Again, the kingdom of heaven is like unto treasure HID in a field; the which when a man hath found, he hideth, and for joy thereof goeth and selleth all that he hath, and buyeth that field.

Matthew 13:44

1. Lord, People Cannot See the Hidden Treasures in Me.

"Lord, people cannot see the hidden treasures in me!"

Well, people cannot see the treasure in you because God has hidden them. God has concealed the potential that He has placed in you.

Every great man of God is like a hidden treasure yet to be revealed. God is the one who sees through the façade and through the outward appearances. All through the Bible, we see that the kingdom consists of hidden things. Your gift is equally hidden.

Your ministry is like a hidden seed! Your ministry is like a seed planted in a large field that is going to become a mighty tree! Expect to grow into a mighty tree as the years go by!

"Another parable put he forth unto them, saying, The kingdom of heaven is like to a grain of mustard seed, which a man took, and sowed in his field: which indeed is the least of all seeds: but when it is grown, it is the greatest among herbs, and becometh a tree, so that the birds of the air come and lodge in the branches thereof" (Matthew 13:31-32).

Your ministry is like a little leaven hidden in a meal! You are like a little leaven that is going to influence the rest of the dough. With time, your influence will spread. With time, your messages will be sought after and your words will be used as wisdom quotes. Although no one takes any notice of you today, you will turn out to be the one who influences all the others.

"Another parable spake he unto them; The kingdom of heaven is like unto leaven, which a woman took, and hid in three measures of meal, till the whole was leavened." (Matthew 13:33)

Your ministry is like a treasure hidden in a field! Once again, the value of your ministry is not obvious today. People will not know what you are worth. As the years go by, people will discover your real worth. As the years go by, you will be appreciated more and more because of the treasure in you.

Years ago, I visited a church that invited me to preach. When I was leaving, they honoured me with what they thought was appropriate. As I continued visiting this church, they seemed to appreciate me much more. At a point, they appreciated me a hundred times more than what they did when I first visited them. Indeed, it takes time for the value of the treasure you carry to be noticed or even appreciated.

"Again, the kingdom of heaven is like unto treasure hid in a field; the which when a man hath found, he hideth, and for joy thereof goeth and selleth all that he hath, and buyeth that field." (Matthew 13:44)

Your ministry is like a goodly pearl that a merchant man will seek out. A merchantman is a man looking for something valuable. He buys it and sells it to people at a much higher price. The merchant man is able to bring out the value of a pearl that he has bought.

One day, people will seek for you. One day, people will consider it a privilege if they can find you and have a few minutes to talk to you. I prophesy that your hidden value will come out as the years go by!

Many times, I have arrived at an airport and been met by an enthusiastic and excited crowd. I have often mused to myself how I passed through the same airport some years before and no one even came to meet me. With time, your value becomes apparent because God has hidden it like He has hidden all the other treasures of ministry.

"Again, the kingdom of heaven is like unto a merchant man, seeking goodly pearls: Who, when he had found one pearl of great price, went and sold all that he had, and bought it" (Matthew 13:45-46).

2. Lord, My Biological Father Cannot See the Gift of God in Me.

And he dreamed yet another dream, and told it his brethren, and said, Behold, I have dreamed a dream more; and, behold, the sun and the moon and the eleven stars made obeisance to me.

AND HE TOLD IT TO HIS FATHER, AND TO HIS BRETHREN: AND HIS FATHER REBUKED HIM, AND SAID UNTO HIM, WHAT IS THIS DREAM THAT THOU HAST DREAMED? Shall I and thy mother and thy brethren indeed come to bow down ourselves to thee to the earth?

Genesis 37:9-10

"Lord, my biological father cannot see the gift of God in me!"

I understand why your biological father cannot see the gift of God in you. Joseph's father rebuked him because he could not understand how he and his other children would one day bow to Joseph. There was a great treasure in Joseph but his biological father could not see it.

God had put commanding wisdom into Joseph's heart! God had put into Joseph the wisdom to lead the greatest nation on earth at the time! Joseph's appointment was as though a prisoner and a refugee had suddenly been made the president of the United States of America.

Unfortunately, your biological father does not see what God sees. Do not be sad that your biological father does not notice or appreciate who you are. When my father was alive, he did not know who I was. He could not see what God had placed in me. By the time my father died, I had not written a single book.

By the time my father died, our church had three branches. He never saw what God was going to do. He prayed for me to be a priest but he had no idea what he was praying for. Do not be worried if your biological father does not see you as God sees you.

48

3. Lord, My Biological Mother Cannot See the Gift of God in Me.

And when he was twelve years old, they went up to Jerusalem after the custom of the feast. And when they had fulfilled the days, as they returned, the child Jesus tarried behind in Jerusalem; and Joseph and his mother knew not of it.

But they, supposing him to have been in the company, went a day's journey; and they sought him among their kinsfolk and acquaintance.

And when they found him not, they turned back again to Jerusalem, seeking him.

And it came to pass, that after three days they found him in the temple, sitting in the midst of the doctors, both hearing them, and asking them questions.

And all that heard him were astonished at his understanding and answers.

And when they saw him, they were amazed: AND HIS MOTHER SAID UNTO HIM, SON, WHY HAST THOU THUS DEALT WITH US? BEHOLD, THY FATHER AND I HAVE SOUGHT THEE SORROWING.

And he said unto them, How is it that ye sought me? Wist ye not that I must be about my Father's business?

And they understood not the saying which he spake unto them.

And he went down with them, and came to Nazareth, and was subject unto them: but his mother kept all these sayings in her heart.

Luke 2:42-51

"Lord, my biological mother cannot see the gift of God in me."

That is true and I understand what is happening. Mary was the mother of Jesus but she had no idea of whom she had brought into the world.

49

How could Mary know that the day her son was born would be celebrated across the whole world for centuries to come?

How could she know that the baby who was sucking her breast was the Saviour of the world?

How could she know that the child who was playing with toys in the garden could raise the dead if He was asked to?

How could she know that her son whom she had sent to school would speak the greatest words ever spoken by a man?

How could Mary know that the blood of her son could wash away the sins of the whole world? Amazing!

Do not be surprised if your biological mother does not see the gift of God in you. Even Mary could not see the gift of God in Jesus.

4. Lord, My Biological Brothers and Sisters Cannot See the Gift of God in Me.

After these things Jesus walked in Galilee: for he would not walk in Jewry, because the Jews sought to kill him.

Now the Jews' feast of tabernacles was at hand.

His brethren therefore said unto him, Depart hence, and go into Judaea, that thy disciples also may see the works that thou doest.

For there is no man that doeth any thing in secret, and he himself seeketh to be known openly. If thou do these things, shew thyself to the world.

For NEITHER DID HIS BRETHREN BELIEVE IN HIM.

John 7:1-5

"Lord, my biological brothers and sisters cannot see the gift of God in me."

Do not be amazed because your relatives do not see the gift of God in your life. Your brothers and sisters who played "Cowboys and Indians", "Police and thief" and "Mummy and

Daddy" with you will not easily see you as the Son of God. Do not be surprised if your brethren do not see the apostolic and prophetic gift in you. Do not be angry with them. With time, they will find out the hidden gift that God placed in you.

5. Lord, My Countrymen Cannot See the Gift of God in Me.

AND HE WENT OUT FROM THENCE, AND CAME INTO HIS OWN COUNTRY; AND HIS DISCIPLES FOLLOW HIM.

And when the sabbath day was come, he began to teach in the synagogue: and many hearing him were astonished, saying, From whence hath this man these things? and what wisdom is this which is given unto him, that even such mighty works are wrought by his hands?

IS NOT THIS THE CARPENTER, THE SON OF MARY, THE BROTHER OF JAMES, AND JOSES, AND OF JUDA, AND SIMON? AND ARE NOT HIS SISTERS HERE WITH US? AND THEY WERE OFFENDED AT HIM.

But Jesus said unto them, A prophet is not without honour, but in his own country, and among his own kin, and in his own house.

And he could there do no mighty work, save that he laid his hands upon a few sick folk, and healed them.

Mark 6:1-5

"Lord, my countrymen cannot see the gift of God in me."

Yes, your countrymen will struggle to see the gift of God in you. Do not be surprised and do not be angry with them.

One day, I was in Brazil for a big church conference. I was honoured to be speaking alongside some of the great names in ministry. Some fellow Ghanaian Christians who happened to live in Brazil passed by the conference and saw what was happening. They made an interesting remark about me at my book stand. They said: "We are amazed at how Bishop Dag Heward-Mills is being honoured here in Brazil." They mused; "He has not been honoured like this in his own country, Ghana."

To not be honoured or recognized by your countrymen is not unusual. Get on with life!

6. Lord, Great Men of God Cannot See the Gift of God in Me.

And the LORD said unto Samuel, How long wilt thou mourn for Saul, seeing I have rejected him from reigning over Israel? fill thine horn with oil, and go, I will send thee to Jesse the Bethlehemite: for I have provided me a king among his sons.

And Samuel said, How can I go? if Saul hear it, he will kill me. And the LORD said, Take an heifer with thee, and say, I am come to sacrifice to the LORD.

And call Jesse to the sacrifice, and I will shew thee what thou shalt do: and thou shalt anoint unto me him whom I name unto thee.

And Samuel did that which the LORD spake, and came to Bethlehem. And the elders of the town trembled at his coming, and said, Comest thou peaceably?

And he said, Peaceably: I am come to sacrifice unto the LORD: sanctify yourselves, and come with me to the sacrifice. And he sanctified Jesse and his sons, and called them to the sacrifice.

And it came to pass, when they were come, that he looked on Eliab, and said, Surely the Lord's anointed is before him.

BUT THE LORD SAID UNTO SAMUEL, LOOK NOT ON HIS COUNTENANCE, OR ON THE HEIGHT OF HIS STATURE; BECAUSE I HAVE REFUSED HIM: FOR THE LORD SEETH NOT AS MAN SEETH; FOR MAN LOOKETH ON THE OUTWARD APPEARANCE, BUT THE LORD LOOKETH ON THE HEART.

1 Samuel 16:1-7

"Lord, great men of God cannot see the gift of God in me."

Do not be worried if great men cannot see the gift of God in you. When Samuel the prophet came to Jesse's house, he made a terrible mistake and chose the wrong person twice. The mistake Samuel made is the mistake that most men of God are still making. They look on the outward appearance and decide whether he is called by God or not. I am aware that men of God are constantly making the same mistake that Samuel made.

One day, I was invited to meet a great man of God but I declined. I said to myself, "If this man meets me, he will not think much of me." I was used to being despised and rejected based on my outward appearances.

7. Lord, I Cannot See the Gift of God in Myself.

And Moses said unto the Lord, O my Lord, I am not eloquent, neither heretofore, nor since thou hast spoken unto thy servant: but I am slow of speech, and of a slow tongue.

Exodus 4: 10

"Lord, I cannot see the gift of God in myself!"

I am not surprised if you cannot see the gift in yourself. Moses could not see the gift of God in himself! What he could see was his slowness of tongue and slowness of speech.

And he said unto him, OH MY LORD, WHEREWITH SHALL I SAVE ISRAEL? BEHOLD, MY FAMILY IS POOR IN MANASSEH, AND I AM THE LEAST IN MY FATHER'S HOUSE.

Judges 6:15

Gideon could also not see the gift of God in himself. There was nothing good him, it seemed. All he could see was that he was a low-class citizen from a poor family.

"Lord, it seems you are the only one who can see the gift me."

Truly, it is the Lord who can see the gift of God in

CHAPTER 4

"Lord, I'm Surprised That You See Such Great Things in Me"

But we have this treasure in earthen vessels, that the excellency of the power may be of God, and not of us.

2 Corinthians 4:7

1. God saw great things in Jacob.

"Lord, I am amazed at how You see great things in me."

a. **God sees that you will be a landowner.** "And, behold, the LORD stood above it, and said, I am the Lord God of Abraham thy father, and the God of Isaac: the land whereon thou liest, to thee will I give it, and to thy seed" (Genesis 28:13).

God sees the land that you will possess. When He speaks to you, it is through eyes that behold your future. I prophesy that you will possess the lands for the kingdom.

b. **God sees you as someone with a lot of children.** "And thy seed shall be as the dust of the earth, ..." (Genesis 28:14).

God sees you as someone who is going to bear much fruit. God sees you as someone who will have many pastors, many church members and many fruits. That is what God sees about you. Whenever He speaks about you, He speaks to you with these things in mind. This will be your story! Much fruit! Many children! Many souls! Great accomplishments!

c. **God sees you as someone whose children will travel all over the world.** "And thy seed shall be as the dust of the earth, and thou shalt spread abroad to the west, and to the east, and to the north, and to the south: and in thee and in thy seed shall all the families of the earth be blessed" (Genesis 28:14).

Your seed will spread abroad. God sees you as someone who will bear fruits to the ends of the earth. Your sons and daughters in ministry will go to the uttermost corners of the world and stand up for Jesus.

2. God saw great things in Joseph.

"Lord, I am amazed at how You see great things in me."

a. **God sees you as the leader of your family.** "And Joseph dreamed a dream, and he told it his brethren: and they hated him yet the more. And he said unto them, Hear, I pray you, this dream which I have dreamed: For, behold, we were binding sheaves in the field, and, lo, my sheaf arose, and also stood upright; and, behold, your sheaves stood round about, and made obeisance to my sheaf" (Genesis 37:5-7).

You may be the youngest in your family. You may be the small boy in your nation. But God sees you as a national hero! You are going to become the most prominent and most important person in your family. That is exactly what happened to Joseph.

b. **God sees you as rising above your contemporaries.** "And Joseph dreamed a dream, and he told it his brethren: and they hated him yet the more. And he said unto them, Hear, I pray you, this dream which I have dreamed: for, behold, we were binding sheaves in the field, and, lo, my sheaf arose, and also stood upright; and, behold, your sheaves stood round about, and made obeisance to my sheaf" (Genesis 37:5-7)

Who are your contemporaries? They are your classmates. Your contemporaries are the people you were in school with. They are the people you grew up with. They are the people who have been around you since your infancy.

God sees you as greater than all these people and He shows you a vision of it all.

God's mind about you is far greater than any thoughts you can have about yourself.

It is time to believe in what God thinks about you!

c. **God sees that you will be prosperous.** "And he said unto them, Hear, I pray you, this dream which I have dreamed: For, behold, we were binding sheaves in the field, and, lo, my sheaf arose, and also stood upright; and, behold, your sheaves stood round about, and made obeisance to my

Lord, I'm Surprised That You See Such Great Things in Me"*

sheaf. And his brethren said to him, shalt thou indeed reign over us? Or shalt thou indeed have dominion over us? And they hated him yet the more for his dreams, and for his words" (Genesis 37:6-8).

God sees your financial greatness! God knows you will not be poor for long. God sees how He is going to provide for you. It is important to see things the way God does.

3. God saw great things in Joshua.

"Lord, I am amazed at how You see great things in me."

a. **God sees you as a great success!** God saw the success of Joshua's campaigns. God saw that Joshua would win war after war and battle after battle. There was no question in God's mind as to whether Joshua would die early in a battle. God saw Joshua finishing his ministry and could speak to him confidently.

Person after person died and Joshua was still there. The instructions that God gave Joshua needed him to be alive to fight many campaigns and displace the enemy. Do not be surprised when God speaks to you about such great things. You will surely live to fulfil all the pleasure of the Lord for your life. "This book of the law shall not depart out of thy mouth; but thou shalt meditate therein day and night, that thou mayest observe to do according to all that is written therein: for then thou shalt make thy way prosperous, and then thou shalt have good success" (Joshua 1:8).

Indeed, God sees that you will win your wars!

You will win every battle that you find yourself in! "Every place that the sole of your foot shall tread upon, that have I given unto you, as I said unto Moses" (Joshua 1:3)

4. God saw great things in Gideon.

"Lord, I am amazed at how You see great things in me."

a. **God sees that you are a mighty man!** I know that you see yourself as a feeble weakling. But that is not how God sees you. God sees you as a powerful person! I know you feel that you are just a little boy or a little girl. That is exactly how Gideon felt.

Gideon was astounded when the angel described him as a mighty man of valour. "There must be some mistake", Gideon thought. But the angel was not making a mistake. The angel was transmitting to Gideon exactly what God saw.

When I became a medical doctor, I did not feel any different. I still felt like a student. I had been a medical student for seven years. But I received news that my name was on the notice board and I was now a medical doctor. I was forced to re-orient my mind and accept that I was no more a "small boy" medical student but a medical doctor. "And the angel of the Lord appeared Unto him, and said unto him, The Lord is with thee, thou mighty man of valour" (Judges 6:12)

b. **God sees you as a saviour of people.** Perhaps you yourself feel that you need saving. God does not see you as somebody who needs to be saved. He rather sees you as someone who will save people. He sees you as someone who will help people! He sees you as someone who will fight to reach the lost at any cost! Rise up and shine for the Lord! He sees you as a saviour of people! "And the Lord looked upon him, and said, go in this thy might, and thou shalt save Israel from the hand of the Midianites: have not I sent thee?" (Judges 6:14).

5. God saw great things in Esther.

"Lord, I am amazed at how You see great things in me."

For if thou altogether holdest thy peace at this time, then shall there enlargement and deliverance arise to the Jews from another place; but thou and thy father's house shall be destroyed: and who knoweth whether thou art come to the kingdom for such a time as this?

Esther 4:14

58

God saw great things in Esther. God sees you as someone through whom enlargement will come. God sees you as someone who must not hold his peace but who must speak continually for the deliverance of God's people.

God sees you as someone through whom deliverance will come.

You may be an insignificant beauty queen!

You may not be a preacher!

You may not be a pastor!

But in spite of what you are, God sees you as a great deliverer and a person through whom enlargement will come to the church.

6. God saw great things in David.

"Lord, I am amazed at how You see great things in me."

a. **God sees you as someone with a good heart.** Men were looking directly at the outward appearance. But God was looking directly at David's heart. People who are looking at your outward appearance and your outward actions are all wrong in the judgment that they make about you. God sees beyond all that and chooses you because of your heart. "But the Lord said unto Samuel, Look not on his countenance, or on the height of his stature; because I have refused him: for the Lord seeth not as man seeth; for man looketh on the outward appearance, but the Lord looketh on the heart" (1 Samuel 16:7)

b. **God sees you as someone who is different from the rest of your brothers.** God sees the difference in you. Indeed, there are differences in people. There are people who will be faithful.

There are people who will be unfaithful at the slightest chance they get.

There are people who will be unfaithful to you because they are under pressure.

There are people who will never yield to any pressure to be unfaithful.

There are real differences between people.

God sees the real differences that exist between you and your brothers! "And Samuel said unto Jesse, Are here all thy children? And he said, There remaineth yet the youngest, and, behold, he keepeth the sheep. And Samuel said unto Jesse, Send and fetch him: for we will not sit down till he come hither. And he sent, and brought him in. Now he was ruddy, and withal of a beautiful countenance, and goodly to look to. And the LORD said, Arise, anoint him: for this is he" (1 Samuel 16:11-12)

c. **God sees you as someone who will do all His will.** It is amazing how God finds you as someone who will do all His will. There are people who will not do the will of God. But God sees through it all and He knows that if He shows you His will, you will do everything He says.

Indeed, there are differences between people. It is God who actually knows the difference between people. When God promotes someone, it is often because He sees a difference which others cannot see. "And when he had removed him, he raised up unto them David to be their king; to whom also he gave testimony, and said, I have found David the son of Jesse, a man after mine own heart, which shall fulfil all my will" (Acts 13:22)

7. **God saw great things in Peter's future.**

And Jesus, walking by the sea of Galilee, saw two brethren, Simon called Peter, and Andrew his brother, casting a net into the sea: for they were fishers.

And he saith unto them, Follow me, and I will make you fishers of men.

And they straightway left their nets, and followed him.

Matthew 4:18-20

God sees you as someone who can be more than a student.

God sees in you something more than fishing in a lake all night long.

God sees you as someone who can do more than selling tilapia to the market women in the area.

God sees you as someone who can deal with human beings.

God sees you as someone who can be a fisher of men.

God sees you as someone who can be a saviour of souls.

God is going to use you in a wonderful way beyond your imagination.

CHAPTER 5

"Lord, I'm Amazed that You Chose Me"

Ye have not chosen me, but I have chosen you, and ordained you, ...

John 15:16

1. Lord, I'm amazed that You foreknew everything.

For whom he did FOREKNOW, he also did predestinate to be conformed to the image of his Son, that he might be the firstborn among many brethren. Moreover whom he did predestinate, them he also called: and whom he called, them he also justified: and whom he justified, them he also glorified.

Romans 8:29-30

God knew everything in advance. Before you were formed in the belly, before you came out of the womb, God knew all about you. Nothing is happening by chance. Because Jeremiah knew that God knew everything, it helped form an unshakeable conviction that his mission was from God.

Then the word of the LORD came unto me, saying, before I formed thee in the belly I knew thee; and before thou camest forth out of the womb I sanctified thee, and I ordained thee a prophet unto the nations.

Jeremiah 1:4-5

For thou hast possessed my reins: thou hast covered me in my mother's womb.

Psalm 139:13

And now, saith the LORD that FORMED ME FROM THE WOMB TO BE HIS SERVANT, to bring Jacob again to him, Though Israel be not gathered, yet shall I be glorious in the eyes of the LORD, and my God shall be my strength.

Isaiah 49:5

God's plans for your life and ministry are based on the fact that He knows everything in advance.

2. Lord, I'm amazed that You have predestined me.

FOR WHOM HE DID FOREKNOW, HE ALSO DID PREDESTINATE to be conformed to the image of his Son, that he might be the firstborn among many brethren.

Moreover whom he did predestinate, them he also called: and whom he called, them he also justified: and whom he justified, them he also glorified.

Romans 8:29-30

You are predestined to do certain things. Many people do not believe in predestination. They say, "Man has a free will and he can decide to accept or reject God. He is not predestined to go either way."

However, the doctrine of predestination is found in the Bible. The doctrine of free will is also in the Bible! Both of these doctrines are real. There are many things that are destined to be because God has stretched forth His hand and decided that they should go that way.

Perhaps, you are predestined to be a priest, a prophet or an evangelist. That is a great blessing. You must be grateful for the call. You must be grateful for the opportunity to be involved in anything for God. It is part of the predestination of your life. As Count Zinzendorf said, "I have but one passion – it is He, it is He alone. The world is the field and the field is the world; and henceforth that country shall be my home where I can be most used in winning souls for Christ." He was filled with the passion to do what he was predestined to do.

3. Lord, I'm amazed that You have made me conform.

For whom he did foreknow, he also did predestinate TO BE CONFORMED TO THE IMAGE OF HIS SON, that he might be the firstborn among many brethren. Moreover whom he did predestinate, them he also called: and whom he called, them he also justified: and whom he justified, them he also glorified.

Romans 8:29-30

"Lord, I'm amazed that you have made me conform to the image of Jesus."

You must not be surprised that God makes you line up with His will. We are all born with a nature that desires the wrong things.

We are born with a nature that likes things we should not like. Our nature is filled with unfortunate longings, cravings and yearnings. These things make every Christian perverted and twisted. I am sure you have wondered how the Lord can use someone like you. I have good news for you!

Those He did foreknow, He also predestined to be conformed to the image of His Son Jesus. The power of God is causing your nature to be changed. He is giving you new attitudes that are born of the Holy Sprit: attitudes of love, joy, peace and kindness!

God has also worked on your will. Your will was damaged by satan and you easily said yes to satan. But when the power of God has worked on you and you are conformed to the image of Jesus, you begin to speak like Jesus and say, "My meat is to do the will of Him that sent me."

You no longer have a weak will that says "Yes" to the silliest of proposals. Your meat is now to do the will of Him that sent you.

4.   Lord, I'm amazed that You have called me.

For whom he did foreknow, he also did predestinate to be conformed to the image of his Son, that he might be the firstborn among many brethren. Moreover whom he did predestinate, them he also CALLED: and whom he called, them he also justified: and whom he justified, them he also glorified.

Romans 8:29-30

God has called you! Yes, He knows you by name. He knows everything about you and yet He selects you out of the crowd and calls you. Be thankful that you are called. Show your gratefulness by being willing, fast and complete in your obedience.

George Muller was determined to show his gratefulness to God by winning souls and serving Jesus. He said, "My business is with all my might to serve my own generation. In doing so I shall best serve the next generation, should the Lord tarry...I have but one life to live on earth and this one life is but a brief life for sowing in comparison with eternity for reaping." What an amazing statement!

I once met a lady who attended a church that had a congregation made up of ninety per cent unmarried girls. It was very difficult for the women in the church to find husbands. Some of the unmarried ladies had to import men, whom they hardly knew, to come and marry them in that country.

One day, a young handsome pastor came to this church, made up of ninety per cent ladies and chose one of them. To my amazement, this lady did not comport herself. Neither did she show that she was grateful. She did not adjust her life to the young potential bridegroom.

One day she told the young man, "Listen, take me as I am. That's who I am. And that is what I am. Take it or leave it!" This lady did not realise that she had been given a great privilege by being selected out of the church that had ninety per cent unmarried ladies. If she had valued the call, the invitation and the proposal that she had received, she would not have said, "Take me the way I am or leave it!"

When God calls you, you cannot tell Him, "Take it or leave it. I will be available after the age of forty." If you value the call of God, you will adjust your life and humbly yield yourself to every thing you need to.

5. Lord, I'm amazed that You have justified me.

For whom he did foreknow, he also did predestinate to be conformed to the image of his Son, that he might be the firstborn among many brethren. Moreover whom he did predestinate, them he also called: and whom he called, them he also justified: and whom he justified, them he also glorified.

Romans 8:29-30

Thank God that He has justified you. This means that you are just as if you never sinned. Your sins are ever before you. The things you did have been done! The thoughts you had have already passed through your mind.

The words you have spoken have already been spoken. There is nothing that can take them back. Like an egg that has fallen on the ground, you have done things that are not easy to reverse. Only God can justify you and make everything new again.

The removal of sin is the greatest miracle of all. I have seen people begging for forgiveness for things they did. It is very difficult for sins to be forgiven and forgotten.

Why is that? People who sinned did what they did when they had the chance to express themselves.

Of course, everyone stops sinning when they are caught. What would they have continued to do if you had not caught them? Everyone knows that the true assessment of a person is what he would do when he has the power to choose. Adam and Eve were neither guilty nor innocent until they had encountered the tree and chosen to disobey God.

How to remove the sin of Adam and Eve is a big question. It demands a huge miracle. A huge miracle is needed to wipe away the act, the memory and the implications of people's sins.

Amazingly, God says that He has justified you. That's a miracle right there!

6.   Lord, I'm amazed that You have glorified me.

For whom he did foreknow, he also did predestinate to be conformed to the image of his Son, that he might be the firstborn among many brethren. Moreover whom he did predestinate, them he also called: and whom he called, them he also justified: and whom he justified, them he also

GLORIFIED.

Romans 8:29-30

To be glorified is to be made nice to God. We are truly born with lots of lust and lots of pride. These are things that do not go well with God. Almighty God hates the spirit of pride and the spirit of lust. Many people do not have what it takes to make us beautiful in the sight of the Lord.

Do you want to know your nature? You are described in detail in the book of Galatians. The things described about you in the book of Galatians are horrible.

Now the works of the flesh are manifest, which are these; Adultery, fornication, uncleanness, lasciviousness, Idolatry, witchcraft, hatred, variance, emulations, wrath, strife, seditions, heresies, envyings, murders, drunkenness, revellings, and such like: of the which I tell you before, as I have also told you in time past, that they which do such things shall not inherit the kingdom of God" (Galatians 5:19-21).

The good news for you is that God has glorified you. He has made you nice. He has made you wonderful. He has made you a different kind of person. He has made you someone who is not selfish, inward looking and vain.

Instead, He has made you someone who cares, someone who is predestined and justified for the ministry. Look at the words of Charles Spurgeon. He was a normal Christian, just like you. The power of God came over him and he walked in his calling. He was no longer selfish, greedy and inward looking. He thought about others and he was a soul winner through and through. He said, "If sinners be damned, at least let them leap to hell over our bodies. If they will perish, let them perish with our arms about their knees. Let no one go there unwarned and unprayed for." (Charles Spurgeon).

"Lord, I am amazed that You have chosen me and destined that I should be glorified like this. Thank You for choosing me! Thank You for knowing in advance! Thank You for predestining

me! Thank You for calling me! Thank You for liking
You for choosing me!

Thanks for reaching! Thanks for choosing! Than
justifying me! And thanks for glorifying me!"

Conclusion

"Lord, I know You need somebody! You can depend on me!
I will be there when You need me.

Thanks for seeing something good in me when I could not
see anything good in myself.

Thanks for seeing something good in me when my own
father, mother, brothers and sisters could not see anything good
in me.

Lord, I am honoured that You would think of me.

Thanks for choosing!

Thanks for reaching!

Lord, I know You need somebody!

You can depend on me!"